SLAM! STARS OF WRESTLING

UNDERTAKER
MASTER OF PAIN

JENNIFER BRINGLE

rosen publishing's
rosen central
New York

Published in 2012 by The Rosen Publishing Group, Inc.
29 East 21st Street, New York, NY 10010

Copyright © 2012 by The Rosen Publishing Group, Inc.

First Edition

All rights reserved. No part of this book may be reproduced in any form without permission in writing from the publisher, except by a reviewer.

Library of Congress Cataloging-in-Publication Data

Bringle, Jennifer.
Undertaker: master of pain/Jennifer Bringle.
    p. cm.—(Slam! stars of wrestling)
Includes bibliographical references and index.
ISBN 978-1-4488-5536-0 (library binding)—
ISBN 978-1-4488-5597-1 (pbk.)—
ISBN 978-1-4488-5598-8 (6-pack)
1. Undertaker, 1965—Juvenile literature. 2. Wrestlers—United States—Biography—Juvenile literature. I. Title.
GV1196.U54B75 2012
796.812092—dc23
[B]
                                                                                    2011022752

Manufactured in the United States of America

CPSIA Compliance Information: Batch #W12YA: For further information, contact Rosen Publishing, New York, New York, at 1-800-237-9932.

CONTENTS

Introduction...4

1 The Birth of a Champion...7

2 The Undertaker Takes the Ring...12

3 The Undertaker in the New Millennium...21

4 The Undertaker Back on Top...30

Timeline...39

Glossary...41

For More Information...43

For Further Reading...45

Bibliography...46

Index...47

4 / **UNDERTAKER:** MASTER OF PAIN

INTRODUCTION

Standing at nearly 7 feet (2.1 meters) tall, dressed in all black with a wide-brimmed hat hanging over his menacing face, the Undertaker strikes fear into the hearts of his opponents when he steps into the ring. Even the toughest of wrestlers knows that when he faces the Undertaker, he's going to have a brawl on his hands.

But the Undertaker, whose real name is Mark Calaway, wasn't always one of the most fearsome wrestlers on the scene. Growing up in Texas, Calaway was just like any other youngster—full of dreams with a love for playing games and sports. Though he was a natural on the basketball court, he could never shake his love for wrestling. Following in the footsteps of his heroes, the Von Erichs (a legendary family of wrestlers from Texas), Calaway gave up a promising basketball career and became a wrestler.

Like most people, he didn't become a success right away. He had to work long and hard, practicing moves and conditioning his massive body, to start finally

Since his humble beginnings in Texas during the 1980s, Mark "the Undertaker" Calaway has been a force in wrestling. Today, he stands as one of the most successful and legendary characters in professional wrestling.

winning. Once he began to win, his alter ego began to take shape—a fearsome and imposing figure, the Undertaker. Taking on the persona of a dark, frightening version of the Old West undertaker—the man responsible for burying the dead—Calaway means business when he steps into the ring. Wrestling as the Undertaker, Calaway became a superstar, winning championships and earning the loyalty of legions of fans.

Today, the Undertaker has overcome injury and adversity to remain one of the biggest and best-known wrestlers in pro wrestling. He continues to grow and improve, and his look and style continue to evolve. But what never changes is his love for wrestling—and his status as one of the sport's greatest legends.

1 THE BIRTH OF A CHAMPION

Although he rules the ring now, striking fear into the hearts of his opponents, the Undertaker was once just a regular kid with big dreams. Pursuing what he loved, he went from being a boy from Texas to one of wrestling's most fearsome competitors.

The Undertaker's Childhood

The Undertaker was born Mark Calaway on March 24, 1965, in Houston, Texas. His parents, Frank and Catherine Calaway, had four other sons as well. Although he would go on to be a professional wrestler, Calaway's first love was basketball. During his years at Houston's Waltrip High School, Calaway played on the school's basketball team. His height—Calaway is 6' 10 ½" (just over 2 m)—made him a natural for the sport, and he became a force on the court.

Calaway began to set his sights on becoming a professional basketball player. Upon graduation in 1983, he went to Angelina College in Lufkin, Texas, on a scholarship earned by his skills on the court. Shortly thereafter, he left Angelina College to attend Texas Wesleyan University in Fort Worth, studying sports management and playing on the school's basketball team. But though he'd played basketball for years, Calaway had a special love for another sport—wrestling. Growing up in Texas, he'd always watched professional wrestling on television, becoming a big fan of the Von Erichs. The Von

UNDERTAKER: MASTER OF PAIN

Mark "the Undertaker" Calaway was born on March 24, 1965, in Houston, Texas. During his younger years in Houston, Calaway became a basketball star at his high school, due to his height and skill on the court.

Erichs were a famous family of professional wrestlers from Texas who won countless championships.

Calaway decided to pursue his love of wrestling while in college. At the same time, his basketball coach wanted him to increase his commitment to the team, which interfered with his wrestling matches and practices. So Calaway decided to quit basketball and pursue wrestling full-time. Around this time, he got a part-time job and ended up quitting college. In the years since, Calaway has expressed regret over never finishing school and getting his degree.

Early Career

Calaway made his professional debut in 1984. He began wrestling as part of World Class Championship Wrestling (WCCW), a Texas-based professional wrestling circuit owned by one of Calaway's heroes, Fritz Von Erich. Wrestling under the name Texas Red, Calaway lost his first match to Bruiser Brody (Frank Goodish), who was known for his wild brawling style. After four years with the WCCW, Calaway left the circuit to join the Continental Wrestling Association, which was affiliated with the National Wrestling Alliance (NWA).

This move proved to be a good one for Calaway, as it led to his first championship as a professional wrestler. Wrestling as the Master of Pain, Calaway faced Jerry "the King" Lawler, defeating him for the USWA Unified World Heavyweight Championship in April 1989. He picked up another title in October of that year, while wrestling under the name the Punisher. This victory was less dramatic, though, as he won the World Championship Wrestling Association (WCWA) Texas Heavyweight Championship after Eric Embry forfeited the title.

During these years, Calaway mostly wrestled in Texas, having yet to make his debut on the national stage. That all changed in late 1989, when he joined World Championship Wrestling (WCW). As a member of the WCW, he wrestled under the name Mean Mark Callous. He partnered with Dangerous Dan Spivey to tag-team wrestle as the Skyscrapers. The Skyscrapers waged a feud with the Road Warriors—Michael "Hawk" Hegstrand and Joseph "Animal" Laurinaitis. But before the feud storyline was completed, Spivey left, and Calaway went back to wrestling on his own.

Wrestling on his own in the WCW, Calaway faced a lot of big-name opponents. During this time, wrestling manager Paul "Paul E. Dangerously" Heyman began guiding Calaway and helped him defeat Johnny Ace at Capital

10 / **UNDERTAKER:** MASTER OF PAIN

In 1989, wrestling as the Master of Pain, Calaway defeated Jerry "the King" Lawler, seen here, to win the USWA Unified World Heavyweight Championship. The win was his first championship as a professional wrestler.

Combat and Brian Pillman at the Clash of the Champions. Calaway wrestled in what was his biggest match to date—a marquee bout against wrestling star Lex Luger for the NWA U.S. Heavyweight Championship at the Great American Bash. But the match would not bring victory for Calaway. Luger pinned him after clotheslining him, taking the victory. The loss was followed by another to NWA World Heavyweight Champion Sting in September 1990. The losses led the WCW to decline to renew Calaway's contract, ending his tenure in the promotion.

After leaving the WCW, Calaway briefly returned to the USWA to wrestle in a tournament to crown the new USWA Unified World Heavyweight champion. During his first match in the tournament, he defeated Bill Dundee. But in the quarterfinals, he lost to Jerry Lawler, the same wrestler he beat in 1989 to win his first USWA Unified World Heavyweight Championship. Not long after the tournament ended, in October 1990, Calaway signed with the World Wrestling Federation (WWF), a move that would change his career forever.

2 The Undertaker Takes the Ring

When Mark Calaway followed his dream of professional wrestling, it took him places he'd never thought he'd go. But even though he had some great successes, wrestling with some of the legendary heroes of the sport, he wanted more. He got it in 1990, when he joined the World Wrestling Federation (WWF).

Breaking into the WWF

Calaway made his debut as Cain the Undertaker in November 1990 during the Survivor Series. His new persona, which would make him legendary, was modeled after a mortician character from an old Western. As the Undertaker, he wore a long, black trench coat, a wide-brimmed black hat, and gloves. Coupled with his towering height, the Undertaker was a menacing figure in the ring. And as the Deadman (another name for his persona), he had another skill: he was immune to pain. He accomplished this by no-selling, or showing no reaction to his opponent's moves.

During the Undertaker's first WWF match, he wrestled as the mystery partner of the Million Dollar Man Ted DiBiase on his Million Dollar Team. It was a four-on-four elimination match with seven other wrestlers. After only one minute, the Undertaker annihilated his opponent, Koko B. Ware, with a finisher: the tombstone piledriver. He also eliminated Dusty Rhodes before being counted out.

After the Survivor Series, the Undertaker dropped "Cain" from his name, becoming simply the Undertaker. At this time, he also switched managers, from Brother Love to Paul Bearer, a ghostly character who carried an urn that held mystic powers that helped the Undertaker. At this time, the Undertaker was a heel, or villain. He would place his defeated opponents, usually jobbers (wrestlers booked to lose a match on purpose), in a body bag and then carry them on his back.

The Undertaker made his WrestleMania debut at WrestleMania VII in March 1991. He quickly got his first win, defeating "Superfly" Jimmy Snuka. This marked the beginning of an undefeated streak, as well as a feud with the Ultimate Warrior. After he attacked the Warrior, he locked him in an airtight casket on the set of Paul Bearer's "Funeral Parlour" interview segment. This led to a year of battles with the Warrior, "Macho Man" Randy Savage, Sid Justice, Sgt. Slaughter, and Hulk Hogan. It culminated with a victory over Hogan to win his first WWF Championship at Survivor Series, becoming the youngest WWF champion in history to date. WWF president Jack Tunney ordered a rematch, which the Undertaker lost, giving the title back to Hogan.

After a disappointing end to a wild first year in the WWF, the Undertaker started his second year in 1992 with big drama. In February of that year, his ally, Jake "the Snake" Roberts, tried to attack "Macho Man" Randy Savage's wife/manager, Miss Elizabeth, with a steel chair. The Undertaker stopped him, which made him a fan favorite for the first time. Shortly thereafter, he defeated Roberts at WrestleMania VIII. Over the next few years, the Undertaker took part in several feuds. He rumbled with Kamala, whom he beat in a casket match. The feuds reached a climax when the Undertaker met WWF champion Yokozuna for a WWF Championship casket match at the 1994 Royal Rumble. During the match, Yokozuna sealed the Undertaker in a casket with the help of other villains, winning the match. Once he did, the Undertaker's spirit appeared from inside the casket on a video screen, warning everyone that he would return.

Return of the Undertaker

WrestleMania X came and went, and the Undertaker remained in his casket. But shortly after WrestleMania X, the Undertaker finally returned after being reintroduced to the WWF by Ted DiBiase. But this "return" was filled with controversy. The Undertaker who returned was not the original Undertaker—he was an impostor played by Brian Lee. But he didn't last long. Dubbed the "Underfaker" by fans, he was defeated by the real Undertaker with a series of tombstone piledrivers during SummerSlam. Then, the Undertaker found revenge against Yokozuna in a rematch in 1995. Another casket match, the rematch went very differently than the first, with the Undertaker coming out on top.

In 1995, the Undertaker battled in a series of feuds, mostly with members of DiBiase's Million Dollar Corporation. Those feuds heated up at WrestleMania XI, when the Undertaker faced off with menacing King Kong Bundy. While the two wrestlers slammed each other in the ring, King Kong Bundy's ally, Kama, stole the Undertaker's urn. Kama taunted him and melted the urn into a large gold necklace before attacking the Undertaker. But the Undertaker got his revenge at SummerSlam, defeating Kama in a casket match. Just a few weeks later, though, the Undertaker injured the orbital bone near his eye and was forced to take time off for surgery and to heal.

Healed from his injury, the Undertaker returned to wrestling at the 1995 Survivor Series, masking his eyes with a phantomlike gray face mask. He wrestled in a four-on-four elimination match as part of the Darkside, with Savio Vega, Fatu, and Henry Godwinn. They took on the Royals (King Mabel,

THE UNDERTAKER VS. MANKIND: FEUD OF FEUDS

Right after WrestleMania XII, the Undertaker's next big feud took shape when Mankind made his debut, interfering with the Undertaker's match against Justin Hawk Bradshaw. Over the next few matches, Mankind attacked the Undertaker again and again, causing him to lose several of them. The feud began to escalate, with the two taking their fights backstage, into the crowd, and into the boiler rooms of different arenas. Mankind cost the Undertaker the WWF Intercontinental Championship at In Your House 8: Beware of Dog, helping champion Goldust get the victory. As a result, the first ever Boiler Room Brawl was booked between the two of them at SummerSlam. During the match, the Undertaker was betrayed by his ally, Paul Bearer, which caused him to lose to Mankind. This took their rivalry to a new level, and at the In Your House 11: Buried Alive match, the Undertaker nearly beat Mankind before being "buried alive." He then returned at the Survivor Series, this time beating Mankind. In 1996, they renewed their rivalry in a match at the King of the Ring. During the match, the Undertaker threw Mankind off the roof of the cell, then chokeslammed him through the roof of the cell, which legitimately knocked Mankind unconscious. The Undertaker finished him off with a tombstone piledriver, cementing his status as the winner of the feud.

Jerry Lawler, Isaac Yankem, and Hunter Hearst Helmsley). The Undertaker controlled most of the match, dominating the Royals and making the first elimination by pinning Lawler after a tombstone piledriver. The Undertaker also eliminated Yankem by performing a tombstone piledriver. Helmsley had to compete against the Undertaker, but he opted to escape the match. As he left the ring, he was chased to the ring by Godwinn, who came out with his slop bucket. As a result, Helmsley climbed the apron. The Undertaker eliminated Helmsley by performing a chokeslam from the apron to the other side of the ring. Mabel dominated the Undertaker at first, but he ended up scaring Mabel, who escaped the ring and got counted out. As a result, the Darkside won the match with the entire team surviving.

In 1996, the Undertaker met Bret Hart in a WWF Championship match at the Royal Rumble. During the match, Diesel interfered by unmasking the Undertaker, causing him to lose. One month later, the Undertaker got his revenge during a match between Diesel and Hart. He dragged Diesel underneath the ring, causing him to lose to Hart. The two met again at WrestleMania XII, where the Undertaker completed his revenge by beating Diesel.

Evolution of the Undertaker

After feuding with several wrestlers, the Undertaker focused on winning a second WWF Championship. He did just that at WrestleMania XIII, defeating Sycho Sid. After the match, Paul Bearer attempted to rejoin with the Undertaker by blackmailing him, threatening to reveal the Undertaker's "biggest secret." The "secret" was that the Undertaker was a murderer who'd burned down his family's funeral home business (where Bearer worked) as a child, killing his parents and younger half-brother. Paul Bearer said he was told this by the Undertaker's half-brother, Kane, who had actually survived and was badly burned and scarred. Bearer said he'd raised Kane after the fire and had him institutionalized, and now he was back, looking for revenge. The Undertaker responded that Kane was a pyromaniac (someone who is obsessed with fire), and he was actually the one who set the fire, and he couldn't have survived.

THE UNDERTAKER TAKES THE RING / **17**

Bret "Hit Man" Hart was one of the wrestlers whom the Undertaker wrestled with in the late 1990s. The two met in the 1996 Royal Rumble match, when the Undertaker interfered with the match between Hart and Diesel.

The Undertaker finally faced Kane in 1997 during the Badd Blood: In Your House match against Shawn Michaels. During the match, Kane stormed into the cell, taking the Undertaker down with his own signature finisher: the tombstone piledriver. This allowed Michaels to pin him and win the match. As their storyline progressed, Kane, along with Paul Bearer, challenged the Undertaker to many fights. But the Undertaker always refused to fight his brother. The brothers briefly formed an alliance when Kane saved the Undertaker from an attack by D-Generation X. But the partnership was cut short when Kane interfered with a casket match versus Michaels, trapping the Undertaker in a casket that he then set on fire. The Undertaker somehow escaped the casket and returned to defeat Kane at WrestleMania XIV. The two had a rematch, the first ever Inferno match, at Unforgiven: In Your House. The Undertaker won by setting Kane's right arm on fire.

The Undertaker met Kane again at Fully Loaded, when he and Stone Cold Steve Austin defeated Kane and Mankind to win the WWF Tag Team Championship. But just two weeks later, they lost to Kane and Mankind at Raw Is War. The Undertaker then became the top contender for the WWF Championship, which Austin held. The two were slated to meet at SummerSlam when the Undertaker and Kane began working together again as brothers. The Undertaker met Austin in SummerSlam but lost and handed Austin his belt back as a show of respect. Later that year, the Undertaker began to take on a villainous persona, and he and Kane began to plot to rid Austin of his title for Vince McMahon. At Breakdown: In Your House, the Undertaker and Kane met Austin in a triple-threat match, where they pinned him after putting him in a double

THE UNDERTAKER TAKES THE RING / **19**

The Undertaker has had a troubled relationship with his brother, Kane. The two have wrestled as allies, but most often, they have squared off as enemies. Their love/hate relationship has gone on for years.

chokeslam, vacating Austin's title as WWF champion. This led to the brothers meeting at Judgment Day: In Your House to compete for the title, with Austin as the special guest referee. During the match, Paul Bearer handed a metal chair to Kane, seemingly to help him beat the Undertaker. But when Kane turned his back, both Bearer and the Undertaker attacked Kane with the chair. The Undertaker pinned Kane, but Austin refused to count the fall, attacked the Undertaker, and counted out both brothers.

The next night, the Undertaker officially became a villain at Raw Is War. He reconciled with Bearer and announced that the two of them would unleash their Ministry of Darkness on the WWF. As part of his announcement, he admitted that he had been the one who set the fire that killed his parents. He then turned his attention back to Austin, hitting him in the head with a shovel during his match with the Rock. He then met Austin at Rock Bottom: In Your House, nearly beating him until Kane interfered to give Austin the win.

As the Undertaker became more involved in his Ministry of Darkness, his villainous persona intensified. He often appeared in a black robe and seated on a throne, and he said he was taking orders from a "higher power." With the help of his minions, he tried to turn other WWF superstars "evil" to recruit them to his side. It was later revealed that his "higher power" was actually Vince McMahon, and after several losses, he cut his relationship with McMahon and his son, Shane.

The 1990s were a major decade for the Undertaker. In addition to a busy wrestling schedule, he had plenty of highs and lows in his personal life. In 1989, he married his first wife, Jodi Lynn, and they had a son, Gunner, born in 1993. But sadly, their marriage ended in 1999. Also in 1999, the Undertaker left the WWF for eight months, due to a groin injury. Just before he was supposed to return in 2000, he was sidelined again with a torn pectoral muscle. These injuries were a taste of future troubles for the Undertaker.

3 The Undertaker in the New Millennium

After a decade of highs and lows that included WWF Championships and sidelining injuries, the Undertaker entered the new millennium as a WWF superstar, as well as one of the league's newest villains. The next decade would be just as exciting for the Undertaker, bringing lots of success and a few setbacks.

Changes for the Undertaker

Once he returned from injuries in 2000, the Undertaker took on a second persona. He abandoned the Gothic mortician-themed attire, his funeral dirge ring music, and allusions to the supernatural. The Undertaker now took on the personality of a biker, riding into the ring on a motorcycle, wearing sunglasses and bandanas. His ring music was now replaced with popular rock songs of the time from artists such as Limp Bizkit and Kid Rock. The one remaining element of his original theme was the characteristic opening bell gong.

Upon his return in, the Undertaker took on his former allies, the members of the McMahon-Helmsley Faction, which caused him to once again become a fan favorite. He also targeted their leader, WWF Champion Triple H. At King of the Ring, the Undertaker teamed with the Rock and Kane to defeat the team of Triple H, Shane McMahon, and Vince McMahon. Afterward, he teamed with Kane to contend for the WWF Tag Team Championship. They defeated Edge and Christian, earning the right to face them the following week for the tag title, which Edge and Christian retained. Kane betrayed the Undertaker by chokeslamming him twice on Raw Is War. This led to another match between the two at SummerSlam, which ended in a no contest as Kane ran from the ring area after the Undertaker removed his mask. The Undertaker then challenged Kurt Angle for the WWF Championship at the Survivor Series. Angle, however, defeated the Undertaker after Kurt switched places with his real-life brother, Eric Angle.

Also in 2000, the Undertaker's personal life began to look up — he married his second wife, Sara. The couple had two daughters, Chasey and Gracie.

In 2001, the Undertaker reunited with Kane as the Brothers of Destruction, contending for the WWF Tag Team Championship. They got a shot at the title at No Way Out, facing Edge and Christian and then the Dudley Boyz in a Tables Match. The Brothers of Destruction dominated the match but lost in the end. The Undertaker then defeated Triple H at WrestleMania X-Seven, where he improved his WrestleMania winning streak to 9-0. He

THE UNDERTAKER IN THE NEW MILLENNIUM / 23

The Undertaker took on a biker persona in 2003, riding into the ring on a motorcycle. He also took on some of his former allies, which helped him become a fan favorite.

and Kane stayed focused on Triple H, who formed a surprise alliance with WWF Champion Stone Cold Steve Austin. The Brothers of Destruction got an opportunity to face Triple H and Austin for their titles. After the Undertaker and Kane acquired the WWF tag title from Edge and Christian, Triple H pinned Kane after attacking him with a sledgehammer at Backlash, where the Brothers of Destruction dropped the title. With Kane injured, the Undertaker feuded briefly with Austin for his WWF Championship, but at Judgment Day, Austin prevailed. At SummerSlam, the Undertaker and Kane defeated Diamond Dallas Page and his partner, Chris Kanyon, in a steel-cage match to win the WWF Tag Team Championship.

Later in 2002, the Undertaker underwent another change in persona, cutting his long hair and becoming a villain again, calling himself "Big Evil." He engaged in feuds with a number of superstars, including the Rock and legendary wrestler Ric Flair and his son, David. But the Undertaker would become a fan favorite once again, beating Hulk Hogan for his fourth world championship. He got caught up in several more feuds and competed in several matches before he disappeared after losing a match due to the interference of Kane.

Return of the Deadman

In the weeks leading up to WrestleMania XX, Kane was haunted by dreams proclaiming the Undertaker's return. At WrestleMania XX, the Undertaker, who'd taken his "Deadman" persona back on and was accompanied by Paul Bearer, returned and defeated Kane. A few months later, Bearer was kidnapped by the Dudley Boyz at the direction of Paul Heyman, who then took "control" of the Undertaker. At the Great American Bash, the Undertaker fought a handicap match against the Dudleys, with the stipulation that if he

THE ZEUS COMPTON CALAWAY SAVE THE ANIMALS FUND

Many wrestling fans may not realize that the Undertaker has a major soft spot for animals. He and his ex-wife Sara (they split in 2007) even started their own animal charity, the Zeus Compton Calaway Save the Animals Fund. In association with the Texas A&M University College of Veterinary Medicine, the charity helps pet owners who cannot afford to pay for life-saving medical care for their pets. They named the charity in honor of their dog, Zeus, a mastiff who developed a rare chronic condition that eventually led to his death in 2004. The Undertaker and his family were devastated over Zeus's death, as they loved him dearly. Knowing the tremendous expense of trying to save a pet, they wanted to do what they could to help others in that situation who did not have the same financial advantages that allowed them to do everything possible to help Zeus. They decided to start the fund to help other pet owners and honor Zeus's memory.

didn't lay down and purposely lose, Heyman would bury Bearer in cement. The Undertaker won and stopped Heyman from burying Bearer, then buried him anyway, explaining that Bearer was merely a liability.

Soon afterward, Randy Orton challenged the Undertaker to a match at WrestleMania XXI, claiming he would end the Undertaker's WrestleMania winning streak. Even with help from his father "Cowboy" Bob Orton, Randy failed, and the Undertaker improved his WrestleMania record to 13-0. At SummerSlam, Orton defeated the Undertaker in a WrestleMania rematch.

Undertaker: *Master of Pain*

The Undertaker and Kane reconciled in 2006 to revive the Brothers of Destruction tag team. They defeated Mr. Kennedy and MVP on *SmackDown*, helping start a feud between the Undertaker and Kennedy.

The storyline intensified as the two taunted each other with caskets, leading to a casket match at No Mercy, in which the Undertaker lost to Randy and his father, "Cowboy" Bob Orton. After the match, the Ortons poured gasoline on the casket and set it on fire. When the charred casket was opened, however, the Undertaker had once again disappeared. He returned during the Survivor Series, emerging from a burning casket. The Undertaker returned to *SmackDown* in early December to haunt Orton and set up a Hell in a Cell match at Armageddon. After winning the match, the Undertaker took a short hiatus from wrestling.

In early 2006, the Undertaker briefly returned at the Royal Rumble. He then lost a match to Kurt Angle at No Way Out, and after the match, he cornered Angle, telling him that he had his number and that he was not finished with him yet. After tangling at another match, the Undertaker then challenged Mark Henry to a casket match at WrestleMania XXII. Henry vowed to end the Undertaker's WrestleMania winning streak, but the Undertaker defeated him to become 14-0, keeping his winning streak alive.

The Undertaker surprised many when he reunited with Kane on *SmackDown* to form the Brothers of Destruction for the first time in five years, defeating Mr. Kennedy and MVP, with whom Kane was feuding at the time. After several more meetings between Kennedy and the Undertaker, the two began a feud that continued into 2007 as Kennedy cost the Undertaker two World Heavyweight Championship opportunities for a championship match at the Royal Rumble.

The Undertaker won his first Royal Rumble match at the 2007 event, becoming the first man to enter the Rumble at number 30 and win the match. After carrying on a long-running feud with Batista, the two battled at the Survivor Series, where Edge returned and interfered to help Batista retain the World Heavyweight Championship. In response to this, the Under-

28 / **UNDERTAKER:** *MASTER OF PAIN*

Kane and the Undertaker also wrestled against each other many times during their careers. Their bitter rivalry has made for some electrifying battles in the ring and has fueled numerous storylines.

The Undertaker in the New Millennium | 29

taker delivered a tombstone piledriver to general manager Vickie Guerrero on the next *SmackDown*, sending her to the hospital.

At No Way Out, the Undertaker defeated Batista, Finlay, the Great Khali, Montel Vontavious Porter, and Big Daddy V in an elimination chamber to become the top contender for Edge's World Heavyweight Championship at WrestleMania XXIV. He defeated Edge at WrestleMania with his "Hell's Gate" submission hold to win his second World Heavyweight Championship and elevate his undefeated streak at WrestleMania to 16-0. In a WrestleMania rematch, the Undertaker defeated Edge again at Backlash to retain the World Heavyweight Championship. Guerrero announced that the Undertaker's "Hell's Gate" was an illegal hold and stripped him of the title. The Undertaker battled Edge for the vacant title at Judgment Day, which he won by count-out. Vickie ordered that the title remain vacant because titles cannot change hands in this way. Edge and the Undertaker faced each other again for the vacant championship at One Night Stand in a Tables, Ladders, and Chairs match, which the Undertaker lost after interference from La Familia. As a result of the stipulation, Undertaker was forced to leave the WWE.

4 The Undertaker Back on Top

As the 2000s decade began to wind to a close, the Undertaker's career was hotter than ever. But a feud with Vickie Guerrero meant that he was exiled from the WWE. His future was uncertain in 2008, but just as he had in the past, the Undertaker overcame adversity to return as a force to be reckoned with in professional wrestling.

Championships and Big Wins

On the July 2008 episode of *SmackDown*, Guerrero announced that she had reinstated the Undertaker and that Edge would face him at SummerSlam. The Undertaker won the match, and after, he chokeslammed Edge from the top of a ladder and through the ring canvas. Following this match, Guerrero tried to apologize to the Undertaker on *SmackDown*, but he told her that he is not the forgiving kind. At Unforgiven, he approached the ring to "take Guerrero's soul" and take her in a casket. The Big Show, who appeared at first to aid the Undertaker, betrayed and assaulted him. As a result of this altercation, the Undertaker and Big Show faced each other in a match at No Mercy, where Big Show knocked the Undertaker out with a punch to the back of the head. But the Undertaker got his revenge at Cyber Sunday, when he defeated the Big Show in a Last Man Standing match. The Undertaker then went on to defeat the Big Show at the Survivor Series in a casket match, ending the feud.

THE UNDERTAKER BACK ON TOP / **31**

At SummerSlam in 2008, the Undertaker made his return to the ring after an extended absence. He faced Edge, defeating him with a dramatic chokeslam from atop a ladder.

At No Way Out, the Undertaker was part of the WWE Championship Elimination Chamber match, which was won by Triple H. He then became embroiled in a feud with Shawn Michaels over his WrestleMania undefeated streak and the fact that the Undertaker had never defeated Michaels in a singles match. The feud culminated in a match at WrestleMania XXV in April 2009. The Undertaker won to extend his WrestleMania streak to a perfect record of 17-0. After WrestleMania, he took a hiatus from wrestling.

After a four-month absence from wrestling, the Undertaker returned at SummerSlam by attacking CM Punk, who had just won the World Heavyweight Championship. This started a feud that continued at Breaking Point, where the Undertaker faced Punk in a submission match. The Undertaker initially won the match with his "Hell's Gate" submission hold, but the match was restarted by *SmackDown* general manager Theodore Long, who ruled that the ban placed on the move by Vickie Guerrero was still in effect. Punk went on to win the match with his anaconda vise when referee Scott Armstrong called for the bell, despite the Undertaker never submitting. At the next *SmackDown*, Long announced that the ban had been officially lifted, after being released from a casket that the Undertaker had apparently placed him in. The feud between the two continued at Hell in a Cell, where the Undertaker beat CM Punk for the World Heavyweight Championship. The Undertaker went on to

THE UNDERTAKER BACK ON TOP | 33

Amid a bitter feud with Shawn Michaels, the Undertaker earned his seventeenth consecutive WrestleMania win, defeating Michaels at WrestleMania XXV in 2009. Afterward, the Undertaker took a temporary leave from wrestling.

successfully defend the title against CM Punk in several rematches. He then faced Batista at TLC: Tables, Ladders & Chairs for the championship, and won when the match was restarted by Long, after Batista had originally won after using a low blow.

At the Elimination Chamber in February 2010, a pyrotechnics malfunction momentarily engulfed the Undertaker in flames during his ring entrance. He was able to continue with his scheduled match, despite getting a burn on his chest from the fireworks. During the match, he lost the World Heavyweight Championship to Chris Jericho after interference from Shawn Michaels. The Undertaker never used the rematch clause that would normally be given to him. The following night, on *Raw*, Michaels claimed that he caused the Undertaker to lose his championship because he wanted to face him at WrestleMania XXVI. The Undertaker agreed to the match on one condition—that Michaels would retire if he lost. As a result, the match was made into a no-disqualification and no-count-out match. At WrestleMania XXVI, the Undertaker defeated Michaels in the "Streak vs. Career" match to extend his WrestleMania winning streak to 18-0 and force Michaels to retire. After the match, the Undertaker shook Michaels's hand as a sign of respect.

Feuds and Injuries

After a hiatus, the Undertaker returned to *SmackDown* on May 28, defeating Rey Mysterio to qualify for a spot in the Fatal 4-Way to compete for the World Heavyweight Championship. During a qualifying match, the Undertaker suffered a concussion, a broken orbital bone, and a broken nose, and he was bleeding profusely by the end of the match. The following week, Kane said that the Undertaker had been found in a vegetative state. This led to a feud between Kane and Mysterio, who both accused the other of

Signature Moves

Throughout his years as a wrestler, the Undertaker became known for several signature moves. These moves made him a star and helped him win some major matches:

Chokeslam—This is a type of body slam in which a wrestler grabs his opponent's neck, lifts him up, and slams him to the mat.

Last ride—This is the Undertaker's version of an elevated powerbomb, in which a wrestler lifts his opponent high by holding on to the opponent and extending his arms up, lifting the opponent up off his shoulders just moments before slamming him down to the mat. This move requires a wrestler to have tremendous strength.

Tombstone piledriver—In this variation of a belly-to-belly piledriver, a wrestler holds his opponent upside down in a belly-to-belly position, then falls to a kneeling position.

Snake eyes—In this move, a wrestler places his opponent stomach down on his shoulder so that they are both facing the same direction. The attacking wrestler then drops the opponent that he has elevated on his shoulder face first into the turnbuckle.

attacking the Undertaker and putting him in the vegetative state.

At SummerSlam, the Undertaker returned to confront Kane and Mysterio, only to be overpowered and tombstoned by Kane. On the September 3 edition of *SmackDown*, Kane challenged the Undertaker to a match at Night of Champions for the World Heavyweight Championship. Kane mocked the Undertaker, calling him weak and threatening to finish him off. At Night of Champions, the Undertaker was indeed defeated by Kane, who won the World Heavyweight Championship by delivering a tombstone to the Undertaker in a No Holds Barred match. On the September 24 episode of *SmackDown*, a casket was rolled to the ring at the end of the show. To the surprise of everyone, Paul Bearer emerged, having reunited with the Undertaker. Bearer looked on as the Undertaker attacked his brother. But Bearer was still just as sneaky as he'd always been, turning on the Undertaker during the Hell in a Cell match against Kane. On the October 15 episode of *SmackDown*, the Undertaker accepted a challenge from Kane for a Buried Alive match at Bragging Rights for the World Heavyweight Championship. The match did not go well for the Undertaker, though, as he lost after being attacked by the Nexus. This match ended the feud between the Undertaker and Kane and ended the

THE UNDERTAKER BACK ON TOP / 37

After two failed marriages, the Undertaker finally met his match in fellow wrestler Michelle McCool. The two married in June 2010 and became one of wrestling's most popular couples.

Undertaker's career, at least for a while, as he took a break to get surgery for a torn rotator cuff in his right shoulder.

Despite injuries and losses, the Undertaker had plenty to celebrate in his personal life when he married fellow wrestler Michelle McCool in June 2010.

In early 2011, he returned to *Raw* after several months' absence that allowed his shoulder injury to heal. His return was interrupted by Triple H, who also made a surprise appearance. The two of them faced off in a tense moment and then stared at the WrestleMania XXVII marquee, which turned out to be an unspoken challenge that the Undertaker accepted. The match was then made official on WWE's Web site, being dubbed a No Holds Barred match. Triple H gave the Undertaker a fight, throwing down three pedigrees and a tombstone piledriver. But the Undertaker prevailed, forcing Triple H to tap out after being locked in Hell's Gate. The win extended the Undertaker's streak to 19-0. Triple H was able to leave under his own power while the Undertaker was taken out on a stretcher when he collapsed. The next night, Triple H showed up on Raw and stated that he expected the Undertaker to be back and that he'd be waiting for him.

The showdown with Triple H was just one of many great fights of the Undertaker's wrestling career. Though he began humbly as just a wrestling fan in Texas, he has risen to the top of the professional wrestling world, becoming one of the sport's most legendary superstars.

TIMELINE

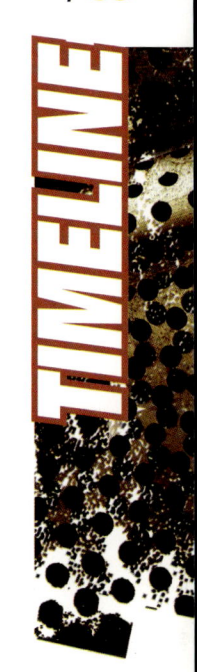

1965 Mark "the Undertaker" Calaway is born.

1984 Calaway starts wrestling in World Class Championship Wrestling (WCCW).

1989 Calaway joins World Championship Wrestling (WCW) as Mean Mark Callous.

1989 Calaway wins the WCWA World Heavyweight Championship.

1989 Calaway marries his first wife, Jodi Lynn.

1990 Calaway signs with the World Wrestling Federation (WWF).

1990 Calaway debuts his persona Cain the Undertaker; later that year, he became known as simply the Undertaker.

1991 The Undertaker wins his first WrestleMania match at WrestleMania VII.

1991 The Undertaker wins his first WWF World Championship.

1993 The Undertaker's son, Gunner, is born.

1997 The Undertaker wins his second WWF World Championship.

1999 The Undertaker wins his third WWF World Championship.

1999 The Undertaker forms the Ministry of Darkness.

2000 The Undertaker marries his second wife, Sara.

2002 The Undertaker wins his fourth WWF World Championship.

2002 The Undertaker's daughter Chasey is born.

2005 The Undertaker's daughter Gracie is born.

2007 The Undertaker wins his first World Heavyweight Championship at WrestleMania XXIII.

2008 The Undertaker wins his second World Heavyweight Championship.

2009 The Undertaker wins his third World Heavyweight Championship.

2010 The Undertaker marries his third wife, fellow wrestler Michelle McCool.

2011 The Undertaker gets his nineteenth straight WrestleMania victory at WrestleMania XXVII.

brawling A style of wrestling in which wrestlers fight in a more street-fighting, no-holds-barred manner that can sometimes lead to injury.

chokeslam A type of body slam in which a wrestler grabs his opponent's neck, lifts him up, and slams him to the mat.

concussion A brain injury that can result in loss of consciousness, headache, memory loss, and even more dangerous results.

elevated powerbomb A move in which a wrestler lifts his opponent high by holding on to the opponent and extending his arms up, lifting the opponent up off his shoulders just moments before slamming him down to the mat.

feud A battle between two or more wrestlers, often involving matches, promos, and angles.

finish The planned end of a match.

finisher A wrestler's signature move that leads to a finish.

interference Involvement by someone who is not part of the match; this may involve distracting or assaulting one or more of the participants in the match.

knockout When a competitor is knocked out by an opponent, usually by a large blow to the head or exhaustion.

no-contest A match that ends in a draw normally due to a legitimate injury where the wrestler cannot continue or because of interference.

piledriver A move in which a wrestler grabs his opponent, turns him upside-down, and drops into a sitting or kneeling position, driving the opponent head-first into the mat.

pyromaniac Someone who is obsessed with fire and the burning of things.

snake eyes A move in which the wrestler places his opponent stomach down on his shoulder so that they are both facing the same direction; the attacking wrestler then drops the opponent that he has elevated on his shoulder face first into the turnbuckle.

tag team A pair of wrestlers working together in a tag-team match (a match that pits two or more teams of wrestlers against one another).

takedown When an opponent is taken to the mat from a standing position.

turnbuckle A device that usually consists of a link with screw threads at both ends that is turned to bring the ends closer together. It is used for tightening a rod or stay.

villain A person guilty or capable of a crime or wickedness.

Extreme Canadian Championship Wrestling (ECCW)

3173 Rae Street
Vancouver, BC V3B 2Y3
Canada
(604) 944-1200
Web site: http://www.eccw.com

The ECCW is a major professional wrestling league in Canada.

Pro Wrestling Illustrated

Kappa Publishing Group
6198 Butler Pike, Suite 200
Blue Bell, PA 19422
(215) 461-0583
Web site: http://www.pwi-online.com

This magazine is dedicated to professional wrestling.

World Wrestling Entertainment (WWE)

1241 East Main Street
Stamford, CT 06902
(203) 352-8600
Web site: http://www.wwe.com

World Wrestling Entertainment (WWE), formerly World Wrestling Federation (WWF), is the main professional wrestling league in the United States.

WWE Magazine

1241 East Main Street
Stamford, CT 06902
(203) 352-8600
Web site: http://www.wwe.com/magazine

WWE Magazine is the official magazine of the WWE and features interviews, photos, and other information about wrestling and wrestlers.

Zeus Compton Calaway Save the Animals Fund
Texas A&M University
College of Veterinary Medicine
Suite 101 - VMA
College Station, TX 77843-4461
Web site: http://www.cvm.tamu.edu/zeusfund

The Zeus Compton Calaway Save the Animals Fund was established to help pet owners bridge the gap between their ability to pay for lifesaving medical treatment and the costs of the procedure.

Web Sites

Due to the changing nature of Internet links, Rosen Publishing has developed an online list of Web sites related to the subject of this book. This site is updated regularly. Please use this link to access the list:

http://www.rosenlinks.com/slam/undr

FOR FURTHER READING

Black, Jake. *The Ultimate Guide to WWE*. New York, NY: Penguin Group, 2011.

Kaelberer, Angie Peterson. *Cool Pro Wrestling Facts*. Mankato, MN: Capstone Press, 2011.

Kaelberer, Angie Peterson. *Stars of Pro Wrestling: Triple H*. Mankato, MN: Capstone Press, 2010.

Loverro, Thom. *The Rise & Fall of ECW: Extreme Championship Wrestling*. New York, NY: Simon & Schuster, 2007.

Miller, Dean. *10 Count Trivia: Events & Championships*. New York, NY: Simon & Schuster, 2008.

O'Shei, Tim. *Stars of Pro Wrestling: Shawn Michaels*. Mankato, MN: Capstone Press, 2010.

O'Shei, Tim. *Stars of Pro Wrestling: Undertaker*. Mankato, MN: Capstone Press, 2009.

Rickard, Mike. *Wrestling's Greatest Moments*. Toronto, ON: ECW Press, 2008.

Roberts, Jeremy. *Showdowns: The Top 20 Rivalries in the Past 20 Years*. New York, NY: Simon & Schuster, 2008.

Robinson, Jon. *Rumble Road: Untold Stories from Outside the Ring*. New York, NY: Simon & Schuster, 2010.

Shields, Brian. *Main Event: WWE in the Raging '80s*. New York, NY: Simon & Schuster, 2006.

Shields, Brian. *WWE Encyclopedia: The Definitive Guide to World Wrestling Entertainment*. New York, NY: DK Publishing, 2009.

Solomon, Brian. *WWE Legends*. New York, NY: Simon & Schuster, 2006.

Sullivan, Kevin. *The WWE Championship: A Look Back at the Rich History of the WWE Championship*. New York, NY: Simon & Schuster, 2010.

West, Tracey. *Brothers of Destruction*. New York, NY: Penguin Group, 2011.

BIBLIOGRAPHY

O'Shei, Tim. *Stars of Pro Wrestling: Undertaker*. Mankato, MN: Capstone Press, 2009.

Shields, Brian. *WWE Encyclopedia: The Definitive Guide to World Wrestling Entertainment*. New York, NY: DK Publishing, 2009.

Sullivan, Kevin. *Undertaker*. New York, NY: DK Publishing, 2009.

WWE. "Undertaker." Retrieved March 10, 2011 (http://www.wwe.com/superstars/smackdown/undertaker).

WWE. "WrestleMania." Retrieved March 10, 2011 (http://www.wwe.com/shows/wrestlemania).

WWE. "WWE Title History." Retrieved March 10, 2011 (http://www.wwe.com/inside/titlehistory).

Zeus Compton Calaway Save the Animals Fund. "Zeus' Story." Retrieved March 10, 2011 (http://www.cvm.tamu.edu/zeusfund/zeusstory.htm).

INDEX

A
Austin, Stone Cold Steve, 18–20, 24

B
Batista, 27, 29, 34
Bearer, Paul, 13, 15, 16, 18, 20, 24, 25, 36
Big Show, 30
Brothers of Destruction, 22, 24, 27
Bundy, King Kong, 14

C
Christian, 21–22, 24

D
Darkside, 14–16
DiBiase, Ted, 12, 14
Diesel, 16
Dudley Boyz, 22, 24

E
Edge, 21–22, 24, 27, 29, 30

G
Guerrero, Vickie, 29, 30, 32

H
Hart, Bret, 16
Heyman, Paul "Paul E. Dangerously," 9, 24–25
Hogan, Hulk, 13, 24

K
Kane, 16–20, 21, 22, 24, 27, 34–36

L
Lawler, Jerry "the King," 9, 11, 15
Long, Theodore, 32, 34
Luger, Lex, 11

M
Mankind, 15, 18
McMahon, Shane, 20, 21
McMahon, Vince, 18, 20, 21
Michaels, Shawn, 18, 32, 34
Ministry of Darkness, 20
Mysterio, Rey, 34–36

O
Orton, Randy, 25–27

P
Punk, CM, 32–34

R
Road Warriors, 9
Roberts, Jake "the Snake," 13
Rock, the, 20, 21, 24
Royals, 14–16

S
Skyscrapers, 9

T

Triple H, 21, 22, 24, 32, 38

U

Ultimate Warrior, 13
Undertaker (Mark Calaway)
    childhood of, 5, 7–8
    early career of, 9–11
    marriages and children of, 20, 22, 38
    professional career of, 12–20, 21–29, 30–38
    signature moves of, 35

Y

Yokozuna, 13, 14

Z

Zeus Compton Calaway Save the Animals Fund, 25

About the Author

Jennifer Bringle has written several books for teens on a variety of subjects. She lives in Greensboro, North Carolina.

Photo Credits

Cover, p. 1 Getty Images; cover (background), p. 1 (background), pp. 4–5 Gaye Gerard/Getty Images; p. 3 (boxing ring), chapter openers graphic (boxing ring) © www.istockphoto.com/Urs Siedentop; p. 8 B. Anthony Stewart/National Geographic/Getty Images; p. 10 Russell Turiak/Getty Images; p. 17 B. Bennett/Getty Images; pp. 19, 26 Jam Media/LatinContent/Getty Images; pp. 22–23 © John Barrett/Globe Photos/ZumaPress.com; pp. 28–29 KMazur/WireImage/Getty Images; p. 31 Orlando Sentinel/McClatchy-Tribune/Getty Images; pp. 32–33 Matt Roberts/Zuma Press/Icon SMI; pp. 36–37 Don Arnold/WireImage/Getty Images; cover background graphic, back cover background graphic, chapter openers background graphic, interior graphics Shutterstock.

Designer: Les Kanturek; Editor: Bethany Bryan; Photo Researcher: Marty Levick